Get the GIGGLES

A First Joke Book

Illustrated by Bronwen Davies

SCHOLASTIC INC.

LEVEL 1 READER

*To my beautiful Hannah and Tommy,
whose giggles fill my heart—BD*

ISBN 978-0-545-54087-2

Text copyright © 2012 by Scholastic Australia Pty.
Illustrations © 2012 by Bronwen Davies.
All rights reserved. Published by Scholastic Inc.
SCHOLASTIC and associated logos are trademarks and/or registered trademarks of Scholastic Inc. This edition published under license from Scholastic Australia Pty Limited. First published by Scholastic Australia Pty Limited in 2012.

12 11 10 9 8   16 17 18 19/0
Printed in the U.S.A.   40
First American printing, May 2014

What time is it when an
elephant sits on your fence?

Time to get a new fence!

What is a pirate's favorite letter?

What kind of button won't undo?

A belly button.

Why don't teddy bears eat much?

Because they're already stuffed.

When is it bad luck to see a black cat?

When you're a mouse!

Why did the banana go to the doctor?

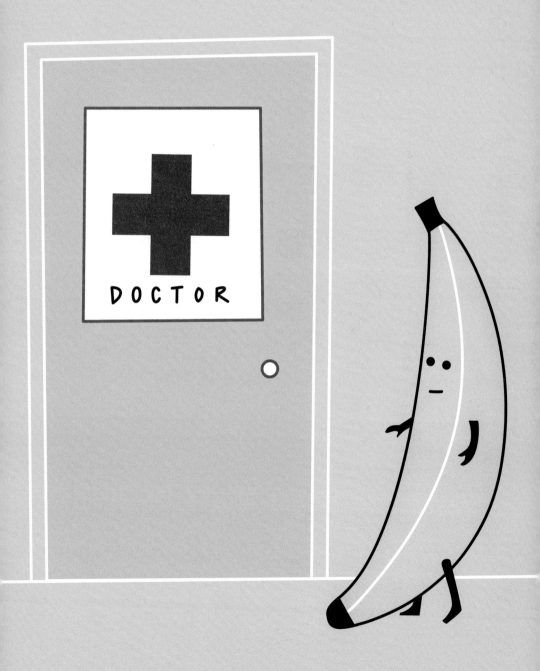

It wasn't peeling well.

He was over the moon!

What has four wheels and flies?

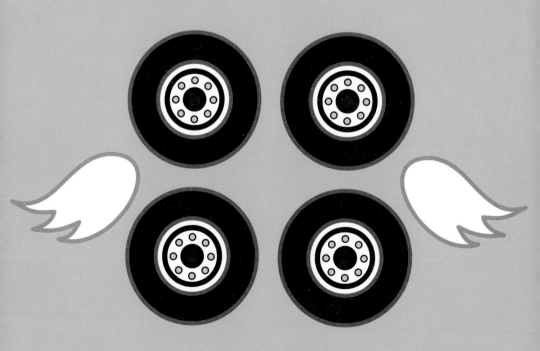

A garbage truck.

What do you call a dinosaur with one eye?

Doyouthinkhesaurus?

Why is it hard to play
cards in the jungle?

There are too many cheetahs.

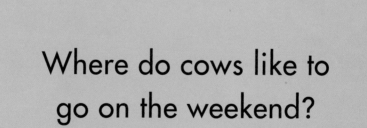

Where do cows like to
go on the weekend?

To the moovies.

What did one snowman
say to the other snowman?

"Do you smell carrots?"

What do you call an electric parrot?

A shockatoo!

What kind of dog
can tell time?

A watch dog.

Why are fish so smart?

MOBY-DICK

Because they live in schools.